Original title:
Where the Succulents Sing

Copyright © 2025 Creative Arts Management OÜ
All rights reserved.

Author: Penelope Hawthorne
ISBN HARDBACK: 978-1-80581-823-6
ISBN PAPERBACK: 978-1-80581-350-7
ISBN EBOOK: 978-1-80581-823-6

Nature's Timid Melodies

In the garden, quite absurd,
A cactus tried to hum a word.
It scratched its spine, and oh the sound,
With all its thorns, no cheer was found.

A lizard danced with flair and grace,
But tripped on roots—it's lost its place!
The leaves all giggled as they sway,
In nature's jest, they laughed all day.

The Song of Life in Parched Places

In a pot, the plants do chant,
A thirsty sage, it's not too plaint.
A rubber tree, with leaves so wide,
Sings to the sun, 'Come take a ride!'

When rain's a guest, they throw a bash,
Each succulent is dressed to flash.
With roots in rhythm, they all sway,
In droll delight, they laugh and play.

The Dance of Resilient Beauty

A barrel cactus spins around,
Its prickly arms, they make no sound.
While aloe sways, it says, 'For me,
The sun is a lively jubilee!'

With dandelion in a hat,
They dance together, oh so flat!
In flower pots, the giggles rise,
Some plants are wise, while others wisecries.

Whispers Amid the Sandy Hills

Beneath the sun, the sand does speak,
A tumbleweed plays hide and seek.
While prickly pear rolls 'round in glee,
It shouts, 'What fun it is to be!'

The lizards laugh, and in a line,
They shiver-shake as if on wine.
In dusty winds, the whispers hum,
'In arid lands, we've made our home!'

The Quiet Elegance of Succulent Souls

In pots they sit, oh so grand,
With tiny leaves that demand a hand.
Whispers of water, a secret shared,
In a world of cacti, they think they're spared.

They sway to the rhythm of a soft, dry breeze,
Claiming their throne with the greatest of ease.
Each little bloom, a colorful jest,
"Don't mind the others, we're simply the best!"

Sunlight Serenades

Under the sun, they bask with glee,
Singing sweet songs, just wait and see!
"Look at us shine, we're practically stars!"
While plotting to take over the jars.

A lizard trots by, gives them a glance,
They giggle and wiggle, oh what a chance!
"Hope you've got shades; it's bright on our throne!"
As they revel in splendor, completely alone.

Echoed Dreams in Dryness

In dusty realms where echoes play,
They dream of rain that's far away.
"Is it today? Do we get a shower?"
But not until then, they revel in power.

With grins of jade, they plan their spree,
"Let's throw a party, just you and me!"
In shimmery pots, they dance on their toes,
Swapping tales of the drought, oh how it grows!

The Gentle Pulse of the Earth

The ground beneath hums a funny tune,
While succulents sway like they're over the moon.
"Do you feel that beat? It's my cactus jam!"
With rhythm and joy, oh, what a glam!

Chasing the sun, but watch out for shade,
A playful turn, it's a hilarious parade.
"Grab your friends, let's dance on the deck!"
Let's raise a pot, and toast with a peck!

A Celebration of Water-Wise Wonders

In the desert sun, they dance and sway,
Charming little jesters, always at play.
With thickened skin, they giggle with glee,
Water-saving masters, wild and free.

A cactus wore a top hat, quite snazzy,
While the aloe did a jig, looking jazzy.
They sip on raindrops, such fancy blokes,
Living life large, taking sips of their jokes.

Under the moon, they throw a grand bash,
With prickly puns and a big, splashy splash.
Succulent humor, oh, what a treat,
Their laughter's contagious, just can't be beat.

Let's toast to the green, the dry, the bold,
To those cheeky plants, worth their weight in gold.
With roots deep in earth and songs on their lips,
They serenade all with their prickly quips.

Voices from the Flora-Bound

In a world of green, they chat away,
Cacti recount tales of the frosty sway.
Succulents gossip, oh what a scene,
About lizards playing cards and being quite mean.

The jade plant giggles, got quite a glow,
Said, 'I told a joke, but it didn't grow!'
While the barrel cactus rolls on the floor,
"Don't leaf me hanging, I've got more in store!"

Their petals lean in, you won't want to miss,
As the agave comments, "Where's my cactus bliss?"
They share their secrets, both funny and grand,
In the garden, the laughter is perfectly planned.

So if you wander where greenery thrives,
Listen closely, hear the jokes come alive.
For in this still haven, there's laughter and cheer,
With plants and their antics, let's all draw near!

Garden Conversations in Succulent Tones

Upon the sun-drenched, sandy floor,
The plants all gather, sharing lore.
A succulent said, 'I'm feeling quite bold!'
While others discussed tales of sun and of cold.

The string of pearls chimed in with a wink,
"Let's plot a heist for that watering drink!"
While the sedum snickered, adjusting its hat,
"I'm just here for laughs, oh, imagine that!"

Each leaf had a story, a quip to share,
About ants that ran off with a nearby chair.
With humor so rich, it would make you grin,
In the garden's embrace, we all fit right in.

As night took its cue, under stars shining bright,
The flora erupted in joy and delight.
For inside each plant, a comic heart beats,
In tales of their antics, everyone meets.

Sweet Songs of the Saguaro

In the heart of the desert, the saguaros hum,
With arms widely stretched, they're never glum.
Singing of sunbeams and cactus ballet,
Their silly moves keep dry blues at bay.

One saguaro claimed, with a mischievous grin,
"I'll outshine the sun if you let me begin!"
The others just chuckled, swaying away,
"Let's dance in the moonlight till the break of day!"

With spines all a-twist, they gather in pride,
Swapping their secrets, no reason to hide.
"Oh, who needs water when jokes flow like wine?"
They laugh under stars, outshining the shine!

So if in the desert, you happen to roam,
Seek the tall cacti, invite them to foam.
For among their tall frames and jovial cheer,
The songs of the saguaros are crystal clear!

Chats with the Leafy Sentinels

In the garden, I hear them chat,
A cactus jokes about a lost hat.
'Could you please take me for a ride?',
'Only if you promise to hold on tight!'

A succulent said with quite a grin,
'Water me gently, let the fun begin!'
They giggle and sway in the summer breeze,
Pretending they're models, oh what a tease!

A jade plant winked, 'I'm not just a drab,'
'Try telling me that while I dab!'
While aloe claims to be the best healer,
But can't cure my fear of the big lawn mower!

As night approaches, they hum and sway,
Chatting on about the sun's ballet.
'Let's plan a party for next week's light,'
I smile as they dance into the night!

Lyrics of Drought-Defying Beauty

Sipping light under a starry quilt,
A euphorbia ponders its built-in guilt.
'Could a cactus join a dancing crew?',
'Only if they promise to keep it cool!'

In the shade, they find their groove,
Singing to the wind, they've got the move.
With a twist and a turn, they sway so fine,
Pineapple thorns lost track of the line!

'Why don't we compete in garden sprout?,'
'As long as we don't have to shout!'
The agave laughs and shakes its head,
'Let's just enjoy this bliss instead!'

With roots so deep and petals bright,
They thrive on laughter under the light.
Chasing droughts and worries away,
They sing their tunes, come what may!

Echoes of Green Beneath the Sun

In a pot of soil, they start the show,
A leafy sage claims it's the star, in tow!
'With roots so deep, I'm bound to shine,'
'But is your charm truly divine?'

A string of pearls rolls its tiny eyes,
'Dude, I'm the trendiest prize!'
They poke fun at the wilting blooms,
'Weakness, my friend, gets you the glooms!'

'How does the sun make you feel so bright?'
'A good tan—better than a fright!'
'Bet I can grow taller in a week,'
'Only if you count your growth streak!'

With laughter rising like the warm day,
They bask in the fun, come what may.
Echoes of joy in their leafy spree,
Where sunlight reigns and they're all free!

Crescendo of the Verdant Spirits

In the corner of the garden fair,
Verdant spirits twirling without a care.
A zesty zinnia bursts, 'Let's have a bash!',
While prickly pals blink, 'Just make a splash!'

Chlorophyll concerts begin to unfold,
Amidst giggles and tales, laughter bold.
'You're looking thirsty,' the mossy one teases,
'But I've got a mini sprinkler for breezes!'

'Why do we all insist on bright style?'
'Because we're the photosynthetic smile!'
The jade chimes in, with a voice so cheery,
'Join my shade party, it's sure to be merry!'

As night cloaks the garden in rhythmic hush,
These leafy folk move with a playful rush.
Singing songs of green under the moon,
Creating a symphony—let the night swoon!

Voices of the Desert Bloom

In the sun, they dance and sway,
Spiky friends with much to say.
Cacti chuckle, oh so bright,
Making shadows in the light.

Lizards giggle, joining in,
A party starts, let's begin!
Prickly pears throw a wild bash,
While agaves make a splash.

A whoop from a yucca, full of cheer,
Tales of the drought, we hold dear.
Succulents twist in a funny knee,
Tickled by the warm, dry breeze.

In the night, moonlight's quilt,
Makes them dance with little guilt.
Nature's jesters, so divine,
In the desert's joyful line.

Echoes from the Garden's Heart

Amidst the blooms, a riddle stirs,
A chubby tortoise twirls and purrs.
Petunias whisper, "Can't you see?"
Dancing roots, a jubilee!

Planters giggle, pots all rolled,
Succulent secrets, not so bold.
Sunflowers gossip with a wink,
"Life's a joke, don't you think?"

Garden hoses have a squirt,
At cacti who wear the prickly shirt.
Jokes take root, they sprout with flair,
As daisies tease without a care.

In moonlit echoes, laughter runs,
Whispers of wind, where giggling fun.
The garden's heart beats, oh so grand,
With every chuckle from the land.

Lullabies of the Arid Land

Underneath the twinkling stars,
Cacti tell tales of their scars.
"Sing us a tune," the moonlight beams,
"Of desert dreams and silly memes."

Chubby hedgehogs snore away,
While agaves sing until the day.
A lullaby in prickly tones,
Where laughter dances, never moans.

In sandy beds, the critters snuggle,
While succulents huddle, give a chuckle.
Whispers of sand, a soft caress,
While nocturnal joys find their rest.

So let the night with humor bloom,
As giggles rise beneath the moon.
In the arid land, a night of cheer,
With playful songs, we hold dear.

The Ballad of the Sun-Kissed Flora

A sunflower beams, full of grace,
Chasing shadows in a race.
Daisies toss their heads and cheer,
"Who needs water? We have beer!"

Prickly pads roll with delight,
While sages spread their arms, ignite.
Thyme has jokes, a fragrant wit,
In the garden, they never quit.

"Oh honey, look!" says the rose to thyme,
"Guess our jokes are out of rhyme!"
They laugh and bloom, a wild show,
Nature's jesters, stealing the flow.

Sun-kissed flora, oh so bright,
Dreams take flight, not out of sight.
With every giggle, roots dig deep,
In this ballad, we forever leap.

Whispers of the Cactus Choir

In a desert dome, they start to hum,
Cacti with rhythm, thighs go numb.
Prickly pops and a thrum of glee,
Swaying in sync, as happy as can be.

A ballad sung under the hot sun,
Needles jabbing, but oh what fun!
They giggle and poke, what a sight to see,
Who knew that plants had such glee?

With a sway and a jig, they dance away,
Not a care for the heat of day.
Throw in a rock, they could start a band,
Cactus composers, oh isn't it grand?

So if you're ever where spines align,
Listen close, hear the tunes divine.
For in the quiet, beneath the stars,
Cactus sing softly, with laughs and guitars.

Melodies Among the Thorns

In a patch of green, a chubby plant,
Singing loudly, sounding quite gallant.
With thorns for wings and a pot for a crown,
He's the king of tunes in his earthen town.

The agave sways, shakes her arms wide,
While aloe laughs, not one to hide.
Together they mingle, an odd old crew,
Making melodies that feel brand new.

Underneath the sun, they frolic about,
Poking fun at the gardener's doubt.
With each little sway, and each joyful cheer,
Those spiky singers have nothing to fear.

So if you wander where spines align,
Watch out for the laughter, it's simply divine.
Amidst all the thorns, there's laughter in bloom,
Turning dry deserts to a lively room.

The Serenade of Silken Leaves

In the calm of dusk, the leaves go sway,
Singing soft songs in a quirky way.
Silken whispers float on the breeze,
As petals blush and giggle with ease.

The drumming of bugs adds to the fun,
A concert under the setting sun.
Rosy succulents in a floral parade,
While dapper daisies join the charade.

They twirled and twinkled, so bright, so bold,
Sharing secrets that never grow old.
In pottery pots, they find their stage,
An audience of critters, a chirpy page.

So tiptoe by when the dusk starts to sing,
Join in the revelry, let laughter take wing.
For in the soft glow of evening's embrace,
The silken leaves dance with effortless grace.

Harmony in Drought

When the ground is dry, and the sun blares high,
Cacti conspire beneath the dry sky.
With each little root, they wiggle and joke,
Making the best of a hot desert cloak.

In the heat of the day, they throw a fiesta,
With salsa and guac from the cactus barista.
A prickly spread, but who would have guessed,
That drought brings laughter and time to jest?

They chirp about rain, while twirling a stem,
These succulent stars, oh how they condemn!
"Here's to the thirst, here's to the cheer,
To dancing in sunshine, with nothing to fear!"

So next time you stroll through arid paths bright,
Remember the cactus party of light.
Even in drought, there's a groove to be found,
In laughter and love, let joy abound!

Melodious Resilience in Bloom

In a pot filled with soil so fine,
A cactus hums a tune divine.
Its spines are sharp, but don't you fret,
It dances lightly, not a single threat.

A succulent sways, oh what a sight,
Under the sun, it shines so bright.
Its leaves all plump, like jelly beans,
It giggles softly in garden scenes.

They prance and twirl, a quirky bunch,
Daring the rabbits — come at their lunch!
The fern rolls its eyes, not impressed at all,
While the aloe suits up for a ball!

In pots like thrones, they rule the day,
With a wink and nod, they laugh and play.
These thriving greens in their happy room,
Declare life's a riot in full bloom.

The Overture of Silken Leaves

In gardens bright, the leaves audition,
For a concert full of wild ambition.
The jade plant strums with all its might,
While the prickly pear takes off in flight.

A symphony of colors burst and blend,
As they strum their chords, the laughter transcends.
The rosette twirls, oh how it prances,
While the rubber plant takes its chances.

All gather 'round for the grand reprise,
The tiny pots can't help but tease.
"Play us a tune, don't leave us bare,
For in our hearts, music fills the air!"

So let them sing, these leaves so spry,
With giggles soft like clouds up high.
A humorous note in a world so brash,
They bloom with laughter, a joyful splash.

Meditations in the Dry Earth

In the desert's heart, where sands do roll,
A resilient bloom claims its goal.
It stares at the sky with unblinking cheer,
And giggles at drought without any fear.

Fuzzy rocks sit in the sweltering heat,
Whispering secrets to bare little feet.
"Stay chill, my friend!" they chuckle and tease,
"Life can be grand, just take it with ease!"

The little pots meditate in delight,
Finding zen in the warm, golden light.
Each leaf a lotus, afloat in the air,
Contemplating snacks that aren't even there.

As the moon peeks in, they pass up a snack,
All giggling at vines that hang on their back.
This arid retreat serves humor in spades,
For laughter yields life, that never fades.

Whispers from the Green Guardians

The potted pals plot mischief galore,
With tiny schemes that you can't ignore.
They huddle together under moon's silver light,
Sharing tall tales of their glorious plight.

"Oh look!" says the sprout, its voice in a rush,
"I once tried to dance, but fell with a crush!"
While the succulent grins, "I tried to roll too,
But slipped on my roots and ended up blue!"

The aloe reassures with a gentle pat,
"No worries, dear friends, we all fall flat.
Together we thrive, in our quirky parade,
With every mistake, a memory made!"

So they whisper sweet secrets, and giggle all night,
These green Guardians of joy, a comical sight.
In leaves and in laughter, they find simple cheer,
Binding their hearts with all that they hear.

Voices Borne on the Wind

Whispers dance in the gentle air,
Cacti giggle, they have flair.
It's a comedy of prickly kin,
With puns that make the daisies spin.

Laughter drips from leaves so bright,
As they tell tales of garden flight.
Chasing shadows, they can't quite catch,
A spineless joke—a real mismatched batch.

Hues of Green in Drought's Embrace

In a dusty patch, they have a ball,
Colorful succulents stand so tall.
With a wink and a sunny grin,
They sip the rain—ha! Not a sin!

They wear their hues like a silly hat,
While the sun sighs, 'Well, how 'bout that?'
Prickles out, they share a joke,
Under a sky that's gone all broke.

The Serenade Beneath the Stars

At night they hum a quirky tune,
Under the moon, they're never marooned.
A chorus of blooms in moonlight's gleam,
As cactus waltz, it's a funny dream.

With flashing lights, the stars join in,
A cosmic laugh—the best of kin.
The universe sways, and all is well,
In the garden's heart, stories swell.

Poetry Planted in Parched Land

In dry earth, they sprout witty lines,
Planting puns among the vines.
A poet's quip in sandy soil,
With giggles, they reap what they toil.

Sipping sunshine, they thrive on cheer,
"I'm upright, but you should see my peer!"
With every joke, their laughter's free,
In parched land, we find glee.

Songs of the Stubborn Blossom

In a pot, the cactus sways,
Singing tales of sunny days.
With arms up high, it starts to dance,
In a prickly, funny romance.

The aloe laughs with all its glee,
"Please water me, can't you see?"
But when it rains, it stalls and pouts,
Claiming drought with all its shouts.

A chubby jade with giddy glee,
Tells the others, "Look at me!"
Round and happy, it lays flat,
Like a plant-sized, jolly cat.

Beneath the sun, a grand display,
Each one stout in its own way.
With tongue in cheek, they all conspire,
To grow taller, never tire.

Conversations with the Unyielding Green

Bushy sage starts to debate,
"I'm the herb that's truly great!"
While thyme excuses with a yawn,
"Without me, you'll be all forlorn!"

The spiky ones roll their eyes,
"Who needs the heat? We're wise!"
Some say, "It's all about the bloom!"
But rooted gems scoff, "We make room!"

A succulent shouts, "I need my space!"
As others giggle, making haste.
"A little water never hurt,
Just don't drown me in that dirt!"

In the garden, tales unfold,
With each debate—a sight to behold.
The stubborn greens sing loud and clear,
In a voice that all can hear.

Echoes in the Desert Garden

In the sand, the plants all chat,
Saying, "Can you believe that?"
A tiny sprout with dreams of flight,
Claiming he will grow all night.

The prickly pears have secrets to share,
"I'm the toughest! Who needs care?"
But when the wind starts to swoosh,
They cling to earth—all in a hush.

The agave spins tales so grand,
Of adventures in that arid land.
"I'll outlast any silly bloom!"
But dances lightly, making room.

Beneath the stars, they sing their tunes,
Laughter echoed under the moons.
As critters join the wild ballet,
In a heartfelt, funny display.

Melodies of Resilient Greens

The jade plant hums with a frown,
"I just can't bear to feel down!"
While string beans dance like they're free,
"Life's too short! Join the spree!"

A troupe of succulents, all in a row,
Making rhythms, putting on a show.
"We're not just pretty—oh no, not us!"
With each note, they gather a fuss.

Lavender joins, sings soft and sweet,
"Don't take life too seriously, take a seat!"
They stew and stew in their sunny glen,
Is there summer laughter once again?

So sing along with spirits bright,
In the garden where it feels just right.
Together, they bloom in joyful cheer,
A melody of greens we hold dear.

The Unfolding of Quiet Blooms

In pots they sit, so green and proud,
Whispering secrets, not too loud.
They stretch their arms for sunlight's glow,
While plotting how high they'll grow.

With blooms that burst and smiles they bring,
They laugh and dance, is that a thing?
A gentle poke from cactus spine,
"Careful now, I'm doing fine!"

The soil is rich with stories old,
Of gardener dreams and battles bold.
They chuckle softly, roots entwined,
"Water us well, don't lose your mind!"

In quirky shapes, they thrive and bend,
Together, they are the finest blend.
With laughter wrapped in petal cheer,
They teach us all to persevere.

Cadence from Earthen Hues

In shades of green, they take the stage,
A dance of roots, a leaf-filled page.
With every sip of morning dew,
They gossip sweetly, just like you.

Tangled tendrils twist and sway,
"Who wore it best?" they often say.
The aloe and cactus share a grin,
As they flaunt their prickles, a stylish win!

From terracotta homes, they plot and scheme,
A succulent life, a gardener's dream.
They tease the sun, beg for rain,
In hilarious antics, there's no shame!

The yarn of life, a tapestry,
Of roots and leaves, wild jubilee.
In silence, they sing a vibrant tune,
Under the glow of a floppy moon.

Celebration of the Stalwart Green

In gardens bright, they stand upright,
With resilience shown in every bite.
They giggle as tickling winds blow,
"Hold on tight, don't let go!"

With colors bold and shapes so neat,
Each takes a turn, a leafy feat.
Bouncing back from every fall,
"Bring on the drought, we'll have a ball!"

The party's here in sunlight's gleam,
With every sip, they chase a dream.
Roots like dancers, wiggling free,
"Join our play, just wait and see!"

A banquet set of earthy fun,
With succulent jokes under the sun.
With laughter wrapped in leafy layers,
They invite us all to join their prayers.

Odes to the Resilient Roots

Beneath the soil, they twist and shout,
In quiet strength, they laugh it out.
With every storm, they take a stand,
In their own way, they're quite unplanned!

Comical greens with sturdy holds,
A twist of fate, a tale retold.
"Not too much sun, are you quite mad?"
They tease the gardener, lightly clad.

In terracotta, they make their home,
Roaming the earth like kings who roam.
With threads of laughter in every root,
They share the joys of sweet pursuit.

So here's to greens that flourish bright,
In silent giggles, they take flight.
With playful hearts, they dream and thrive,
In every pot, they're truly alive!

Singing in the Sun's Embrace

In the garden of green, they sway so free,
Little plants with a quirky glee.
Basking in rays, they wiggle and twist,
Who knew cactus could dance like this?

With pep in their steps, they greet the day,
A prickly parade, come join the play.
Sipping on sunshine, a drink so divine,
They giggle and snicker 'til the end of the line.

Stems standing tall, yet roots made of gold,
Whispering secrets of stories untold.
When winds come a-calling, they shake and they jive,
Making the desert feel quite alive!

In this sun-soaked tale, we hum and we sing,
Kooky little plants, oh what joy they bring!
With laughter in shades of lively green hues,
Dance on, silly succulents, we can't help but snooze!

The Closest Friends of Arid Lands

Meet the duo in the bright, hot clime,
A pair of succulents, oh so sublime.
One's a little round, the other's quite tall,
In this sandy space, they always have a ball.

Sharing their stories, they giggle and grunt,
Trading their secrets, a succulent hunt.
One's full of spines, the other a charm,
In their prickly embrace, they mean no harm.

They swap tales of rain, of sun, and of shade,
Living life boldly, no moment delayed.
Through hardships and droughts, they stand side by side,
Two friends in the sun, their joy can't be denied!

In the vast, dry land where not much survives,
These two hearty pals truly thrive.
With a wink and a twist, they march on ahead,
In friendship so strong, fears are easily shed!

Tales of Succulent Depths

In a pot that's well-loved, a story unfolds,
Of a cactus so bright, and its friend, oh, so bold.
Whispers of moisture from roots deep below,
They share silly giggles each time they grow.

Adventures in dust, and battles with heat,
A tale of mischief, where laughter's the treat.
With each new sprout, they throw a grand bash,
As tiny green buds dance and sprawl with panache.

Oh, the tales they tell of the critters they meet,
A lizard that twirled, and a snail on retreat.
In the depths of the soil, they send out their dreams,
Beneath the sun's glow, life's never as it seems.

Armed with good humor and the sun's warm embrace,
They twirl every day in their whimsical space.
For life in the garden is a giggly affair,
With each little bloom, there's joy in the air!

The Sounds of Sandy Sanctuary

In the sandy sanctuary where critters all roam,
The succulents chatter, 'Tis a glorious home!
They wiggle their leaves, making rustles and squeaks,
In this patch of paradise, humor peaks!

A lizard walks by with a wobbly dance,
While round little pebbles all join in the prance.
The whispers of wind give a tickle to their blooms,
Sandy sounds giggle in the bright sunlit rooms.

Together they banter, a colorful crew,
Sharing tales of the droughts, the storms, and the dew.
With such jolly sounds, who could ever resist?
A melody formed in a green, leafy mist.

In the heart of the heat, where the sandy winds blow,
The plants sing their songs, oh, how merry they flow!
With giggles and rustles, they keep spirits high,
In this sanctuary of joy, under ever-blue sky.

Secrets of the Succulent Symphony

In pots so bright, they sway with glee,
Their laughter loud, you must agree.
With every sip of morning dew,
They croon sweet tunes, a lively crew.

Prickly pears join in the fun,
With jokes that make the cactus run.
The aloe winks with gelled delight,
Singing softly through the night.

The jade plants jive in sunlit rays,
While terracotta eaves drop their praise.
In harmony, they rock the scene,
A quirky band, so evergreen.

So come on down, don't miss the show,
Where leaf and laughter freely flow.
In this green haven, joy takes flight,
With every song, we feel the light.

Songs from the Fleshy Leaves

Plump and proud, they flap about,
With chubby faces, they sing out loud.
From prickly toes to rounded tops,
Their harmony just never stops.

Each leaf a note, so rich and round,
In their fleshy realm, sweet tunes abound.
The melons laugh with vibrant cheer,
As they sway around without a fear.

Cacti tap dance, all in a line,
While succulents groove to the sunshine.
With laughter bright as the noon-day glow,
Their musical garden steals the show.

So pull up a chair, and join the spree,
The concert grows, just wait and see.
Under the moon, they take a bow,
Creating joy, right here and now.

The Heartbeat of the Arid Landscape

In the dry land, a funny beat,
A succulent band with nimble feet.
They shimmy and shake, oh what a sight,
In the desert sun, they dance with might.

The spiky ones sway side to side,
With a prickle here, don't let it slide.
They croon with glee, as dry winds sigh,
And even tumbleweeds roll by.

When night falls soft, the stars appear,
They share their secrets, loud and clear.
The agave's grin leads the refrain,
In a watercolor world, they leave a stain.

Come join the fun, don't be shy now,
Their melodies make you want to wow.
In this dry symphony, laughter rings,
With every note, joy surely springs.

An Ode to Hardy Roots

Oh hardy roots in soil so deep,
You tickle the earth while the world's asleep.
They gossip low, in whispers sly,
As prissy plants reach for the sky.

They show us strength in every twist,
While others struggle—oh, how they persist!
With laughter bubbling from deep below,
These sturdy souls steal the show.

In drought or rain, they stand their ground,
In this green kingdom, joy is found.
And though they're tough, they can be fun,
Dancing in shadows, away from the sun.

So raise a glass to roots so bold,
In a world of green, their stories told.
With each deep laugh, a lesson learned,
In nature's heart, our love returned.

The Portrait of a Restless Sage

A cactus plotted by the gate,
He tells each guest they must wait.
With a spine that pricks, he gives a grin,
"Let's discuss the weather, let the fun begin!"

In his pot, he likes to muse,
Bantering with the roses, refusing the blues.
"Why are we all here in this clay?"
"Why not measure laughter, come what may?"

With wisdom that's drawn from dry days gone,
His thoughts flow like water, but his vase is a con.
"Finding peace is easy," he snickers aloud,
It's all just a game in this floral crowd.

So here sits our sage with his lopsided glee,
He laughs at the world while sipping his tea.
"Life's just a thorny adventure to take,
Invite all the weeds, for goodness' sake!"

Hums of the Hardy Blooms

In a greenhouse joke-telling session,
The blooms compete for the best expression.
You'd laugh till you wilt at their witty retort,
As petunias whisper, "We've got the best sport!"

"Oh darling, you're looking quite dapper today,"
A daisy remarks in a curious way.
"Hiding from bees, or just going for flair?"
"The sweeter the nectar, the more I declare!"

With clinking of pots, they raise a toast,
To the chap who forgot to water them most.
"Cheers to the dry spell, we'll never complain,
Just let us wiggle and roll in the rain!"

So hummed the hardy with giggles and cheer,
Their plays on the sun, just a seasonal sphere.
"Let's dance with the shadows, under moonlight's gleam,
For life's a wild garden, the best kind of dream!"

Voices of the Thirsty Artisans

Gather 'round, you thirsty crew,
We'll sculpt the skies in shades of blue.
With paintbrushes made from silly vines,
Each stroke a giggle in playful designs.

A succulent whispered a cheeky rhyme,
"Water me, please, I'm simply sublime!"
While the aloe chuckled, "Just take a sip,
I'm not an artist, but I'll make you flip!"

With clay all over, a muddy delight,
They sculpted a pot that was quite a sight.
"Is it modern art or just a new trend?
Let's argue over it, that's how we extend!"

So onward they went, these crafty folks,
Beneath the sun, sharing jovial jokes.
"Who needs a canvas? We'll just uplift,
Our laughter's enough, and that's our true gift!"

A Symphony of Succulent Dreams

A symphony starts in the garden tonight,
With strings of the ferns and the wind's pure light.
The bees keep the rhythm, the petals align,
Creating a concert that's simply divine.

"Now the prickly ones, please take the lead,
Show us your flair with a flamboyant deed!"
The juggle of jades danced to the beat,
Even the stones tapped their rhythm so sweet.

The laughter of blooms in perfect accord,
Each note a giggle, a harmonious chord.
"Don't miss the encore, it's coming real fast,
With succulence singing to enjoy every blast!"

So let's join the show in this boisterous sway,
With humor and joy, we'll dance and play.
For life's just a melody, under the sun's beams,
In the garden's embrace, we find our sweet dreams!

Resonance in the Arid Air

In the desert's warm embrace,
Cacti laugh and twirl with grace.
Their spines are sharp, but they don't care,
They serenade the sun-soaked air.

Lizards join in, with tiny toes,
As they dance beneath the rose.
A tumbleweed joins in the fray,
Rolling with giggles, bright and gay.

The yuccas sway like they're in a show,
Feeling cool with the soft winds' blow.
Silly shadows join the spree,
Playing hide and seek under the tree.

And when the night falls, stars peek through,
The silent plants hum a tune or two.
With laughter echoing through the land,
The arid air is simply grand!

Natural Chorus of the Xerophytes

In pots so small, the prickles tease,
With laughter floating on the breeze.
Succulent songs, a quirky choir,
Who knew dry plants could inspire?

Aloe winks as she takes the stage,
While Geraniums turn the next page.
The shadows dance, they leap, they swing,
Making it clear they own this thing.

A giggling flower, quite absurd,
Says, "Let's have fun, forget the world!"
Underneath the moon's warm light,
The desert blooms come alive tonight!

So grab a drink, and join the fun,
As silly plants bask in the sun.
With every rustle, laugh anew,
In nature's band, we find our crew!

The Dance of Drought-Defying Flora

Prickly pear fluffed up with pride,
Twirling slowly, can't be denied.
Not a drop of water near,
But still they twist without a fear.

Teeny tendrils shimmy, sway,
Desert dancing, come what may.
Who could guess these green delights,
Would throw such wild and wacky nights?

A bromeliad with a flair for fun,
Starts a waltz beneath the sun.
Bouncing buds, where laughter swells,
The cacti echo with their yells.

Under starlight, the show begins,
Each leaf a jokester, none of them sins.
With giggles and grins while night awakes,
Drought-defying, as daylight breaks!

Echoing Between Prickles

In the garden's sunny nook,
Echoes of mirth, come take a look.
Little spines wave, making cheer,
As nature's humor draws us near.

Potted plants share silly tales,
Of desert winds and tricky gales.
Cacti jest with every poke,
While laughter lifts like morning smoke.

A sagebrush joins, hip and sly,
With giggles soaring to the sky.
Each tuft of grass, a stand-up act,
In a world that's dry, but oh so packed!

With every breeze and friendly tease,
The plants remind us, with such ease.
In prickly laughter, spirits soar,
Together we dance, forevermore!

The Calm Between the Cacti

In a garden of spikes, laughter blooms,
Chattering plants dispel all glooms.
Cacti wear hats, a prickly parade,
Giggling in sunlight, no plans to fade.

Sipping water from a tiny cup,
Cheering on friends as they grow up.
A senorita in bloom, doing a jig,
Amidst the dry soil, she's dancing big!

A lizard joins in with a wiggly tail,
As the sun sets low, their jokes unveil.
In the calm of the green, a party starts,
With every twist and turn, it cheers our hearts.

So here's to the cacti, the spiky crew,
In their desert delight, there's fun to pursue.
With laughter of leaves, and chirps in the air,
They remind us that joy is all we can share.

Tuning into Flora's Breath

The morning hum with a giggle or two,
As daisies whisper 'Hey, how about you?'
Palms clap together, swaying with glee,
Conducting the breeze for a light symphony.

Oh, what a tune from the flowers so bold,
Their secrets and rhymes, a joy to behold.
Grasshoppers join in, with a hop and a squeak,
Making melodies bright, so fun and unique.

A sunflower strums on a stem like a bass,
While violets croon, bringing smiles to each face.
In this green concert, the giggles are rife,
Each petal a note in the song of sweet life.

So tune in, dear friends, to this floral delight,
Where chuckles abound in the warm summer light.
With colors and laughter in perfect array,
Let's celebrate flora, come join the ballet!

Sacred Melodies of the Sun-Kissed Veldt

Under a sun that's warm and bright,
The wildebeests dance, what a sight!
Zebras are striped, their laughter in line,
Giggling at shadows, all looking divine.

With echoes of hoots from the trees up high,
A chorus of critters takes to the sky.
In the breeze, the grasses sway,
Making tunes that frolic and play.

Fluffy clouds join in for a whimsical show,
Painting the sky with a soft, merry glow.
The rhythm of hoofbeats, and nature's own song,
Makes even the shyest feel they belong.

So gather around for this grand celebration,
In the sun-kissed veldt, a joyful creation.
With each silly squeal, we'll dance to the beat,
For laughter and love make this story complete!

The Rhymes of Resilience

In the cracks of the earth, where the tough grow,
Lives a sprightly plant, with a fresh, funny show.
Bamboo stands tall, all dashed with delight,
While succulents giggle through day and through night.

With roots that are clever and stems that won't bend,
They share their stories with every dear friend.
A tumbleweed rolls by with a cheeky grin,
Chiming in laughter, it's ready to spin.

Oh, the magic they weave, these plants of great charm,
Wrap us in warmth, like a buttery balm.
Through droughts they dance, in the breeze they may twirl,
Life's punchlines revealed in a leafy swirl.

So raise a glass to these warriors of green,
Their humor and strength are the sights to be seen.
With joy that defies every struggle and strife,
They remind us resilience is part of this life!

Chants Through the Sandy Soil

In a garden of giggles, plants pretend,
Singing to soil, they start to bend.
Cacti in costumes, all dressed up tight,
Wobbling and jiggling, what a sight!

A worm in a top hat, so dapper and spry,
Winks at the daisies, who give a sly sigh.
"Let's have a party, we'll dance through the night,
With roots all entwined, what a delight!"

A sunflower spins with a twist and a twirl,
While succulents giggle, their leaves all a-whirl.
The moon peeks in, with a curious grin,
"Do I join this jamboree? Where do I begin?"

In sandy domains, where laughter erupts,
Every plant's secret, they joyfully disrupt.
So join in the fun, where the silly things grow,
Just don't step on the roots, or you'll steal the show!

Crescendo of Colorful Spines

In gardens of green, where spines dance bold,
Each hue a story, each petal, a gold.
The prickly performers, a comedy crew,
Waving bright limbs, in a colorful hue.

"Look at me!" screams a chubby agave,
"I'm sharper than knives; I'm the spiny suave!"
They giggle and jiggle, those quirky old thorns,
As butterflies waltz in their sweet, goofy swarms.

With laughter like sunshine, they sway and they sway,
They invite all the critters, for a fun-filled day.
"Join our fiesta, we're spiky yet bright,
Trust us, we're friendly, just don't hug too tight!"

As shadows grow longer, they hum a sweet tune,
Under the watch of a giggling moon.
In the crescendo of colors, a joy-filled brigade,
They paint the night sky in a shimmering parade!

A Symphony of Stillness

In a quiet corner, the plants conspire,
Stillness is music, their roots never tire.
A melodious hum through the leaves softly plays,
As whispers of laughter stretch out through the rays.

An old cactus chuckles, "I'm wiser than trees,
With spines for protection, I do as I please!"
A stone joins the convo, perched close by,
"Just watch where you're poking; the cacti will cry!"

With no need for drama, they bask in the sun,
A symphony played when the day is all done.
No movements too frantic, just a chill kind of vibe,
They laugh at the rush, with roots as their tribe.

Calm like the desert, where stillness reigns bold,
Their giggles are secrets, and tales to be told.
In this world of silence, let's relish the cheer,
For the joy of the quiet is what brings us near!

Harmonies of the Thirsty Earth

Beneath the dry surface, the roots go deep,
Thirsty for laughter, in sun, they leap.
With every small raindrop, they burst into song,
A jig of delight where water belongs.

"Water's for dancing, so bring on the rain!"
The cacti all giggle, and say, "Let's complain!"
"Why can't we get something, we're thirsty, you see?
Let's reach for the clouds, just a sip of glee!"

A pond joined the party, reflecting the fun,
While frogs croaked in harmony, "Oh, look! Here comes one!"
The plants and the critters, all sprouted up high,
Together they crooned, reaching up to the sky.

With rhythms of moisture, they sway in delight,
Harmonies of play, all through the night.
In the thirsty earth's heart, where the laughter is free,
Join in the jubilee, plant, critter, and bee!

Harmonies in the Cactus Grove

In the grove, the cacti prance,
With a jig that's quite a chance.
They sway and bop with all their might,
Singing tunes till late at night.

Spines do tickle when they sway,
Quirky tunes, come join the fray!
They poke fun with every beat,
Dance on sand, oh what a treat!

Bouncing shadows in the lights,
Cacti forming band delights.
Who knew they had secret gigs?
Their music's filled with cactus jigs!

Underneath the desert star,
Cacti dream of being a star.
With a flourish, they all grin,
In this dance, let's all jump in!

Whispers of Prickly Pears

Around the pears, a chatter brews,
Gossip quiet in the hues.
"Did you hear about that bloom?"
"Sure, it danced away with doom!"

Each pear wears a silly face,
Spiky laughs in this odd place.
Fruits are giggling full of glee,
As whispers bounce from tree to tree.

"Watch your step, oh here they come!"
"Prickly jokes can be quite dumb!"
Laughter echoes through the field,
Their humor, oh, it won't yield!

As moonlight graces evening air,
Prickly pears just do not care.
With every joke that they share,
Giggles circle everywhere!

Serenade of the Sandy Soil

Underneath the sandy rays,
Soil hums in a funny craze.
Tickling roots with every beat,
Dancing worms, oh such a feat!

The sand makes whispers, soft and sly,
"Hey, look at me, I'm quite spry!"
Bouncy pebbles join the tune,
As laughter swirls beneath the moon.

"Oh! Here comes a hungry bug!"
"Watch it dance and give a shrug!"
Soil chuckles, tenders do sway,
In this earthy cabaret!

With every giggle, seeds awake,
Sandy soil for goodness' sake!
Here's to laughter from below,
Singing seeds as wild winds blow!

Lullabies Among the Succulent Shadows

In the shade where shadows lie,
Succulents murmur, oh so sly.
"Let me tell you a funny tale,"
"Of a cactus who tried to sail!"

With every leaf, a giggle grows,
Echoing through the gentle prose.
"Paddling pots, he made quite waves,
But forgot how to find the caves!"

Oh! The shadows lighthearted scheme,
Lulling all into a dream.
"Let's create a party vibe!"
"Where our silliness will thrive!"

When night drapes her velvet cloak,
Each succulent begins to poke.
As lullabies weave through the air,
They giggle still without a care!

Songs of Resilience and Grace

In the corner of my garden, oh so bright,
A cactus danced, it was quite a sight.
Sipping water like a fancy drink,
"Cheers!" it said, with a little wink.

A succulent smiled, spreading great cheer,
Giggling at raindrops, drawing them near.
With arms wide open, they'd hum a tune,
Under the watchful eye of the moon.

A chubby jade plant rocked in its pot,
Shaking its leaves like it was quite hot.
"Join the party, don't be shy!"
Even the stones wished to give it a try!

In this oasis, laughter's the song,
Even the soil couldn't help but sing along.
So come for a visit, stay for the fun,
In a world where plants know how to run!

Desert Harmony in Green

Under a sky that glows so blue,
Laughter erupts, bringing joy anew.
Bouncing along like a playful breeze,
Cacti do the cha-cha, oh so at ease.

In the sand, where the tumbleweed roams,
A succulent band calls this place home.
With pots for drums and leaves for guitars,
They serenade the twinkling stars.

The sun can be hot, but spirits stay cool,
Each prickly friend breaks the gardening rule.
"Let's have a picnic!" one keenly exclaimed,
"Just don't forget, I'm not to be blamed!"

A party of flora, both clever and spry,
Giggling together as the days flit by.
Desert dweller's banter, a sight to behold,
In shades of green, their stories unfold.

Cadence of the Clay

In a pot stacked high, the rebels conspire,
With dirt and charm, they never tire.
"Let's break out!" cheered a daring aloe,
As hubby cactus rolled, "Just let it flow!"

In the rhythm of roots, they croon a tune,
Swaying like dancers beneath the moon.
"More sun!" shouted one, "But not too much,
We're delicate darlings; we prefer a touch!"

A holiday party for sprouts far and wide,
Wiggling and jiggling, in all their pride.
"Grab your sunscreen!" a jade plant did yell,
For this gathering, we'll rise and excel!

With laughter aplenty and stories to tell,
Even the soil wished it could ring a bell.
So join in the fun, in this joyful display,
The cadence of clay, come dance today!

Rhythms Beneath the Sun

In the midday heat, a laughter parade,
Succulents strike poses, show off their jade.
A plump little guy shouted, "Look at me!"
With each silly grin, they all felt free.

In the garden's embrace, a talent show,
"Watch my twist!" cried a verdant agave,
"Can you do this?" a crass plant retorted,
"Take a chill pill, relax, it's all imported!"

With roots intertwined, they started a chant,
"Who's got the best spines in this plant!"
It turned into laughter, dancing, and song,
In the midst of clay, where all belong.

So come one, come all, let's celebrate play,
With humor and love driving worries away.
Under the sun, their spirits will soar,
In the rhythm of laughter, forevermore!

The Ballad of Thrive and Survive

In the corner of the yard, quite spry,
A cactus danced, oh my! oh my!
With arms akimbo and a grin so wide,
He jived with peppers, side by side.

The succulents laughed, oh what a glee,
Debating who could be the wittiest, you see.
Aloe joked about her healing flair,
While jade plant bragged of her luscious hair.

Potting soil was a scattered mess,
Each plant claimed they had the best dress.
With terracotta pots as fancy hats,
They twirled around like garden brats.

In endless sunshine, their spirits climb,
The camaraderie blooms with a cheeky rhyme.
As night falls, they snicker and sway,
Who knew plants could have such fun all day?

Paintings in the Sunlit Garden

In a garden bright, oh what a scene,
Succulents pose like they're meant to be seen.
A rose joined in with a cheeky wink,
Claiming her petals could outshine pink.

Cacti wore shades to strut and boast,
Sipping sunshine like it was a toast.
The snapdragons giggled at this grand show,
While daisies rolled eyes—oh, what a flow!

Each plant on display, a work of art,
With colors so vivid, they'd steal your heart.
They whispered secrets, shared a jest,
In this artful patch, they felt the best.

A daffodil chimed in with a tune,
Creating laughter beneath the moon.
In the sunlit garden, they sing with cheer,
Painting a world, oh so dear!

Layers of Life in Succulent Silhouettes

Beneath the fragrant morning dew,
Succulents pondered what to do.
With layers thick, they shared a thought,
Could they be the juiciest plot?

Echeveria rolled her eyes with glee,
"I'm thicker than you, come take a peek!"
While sedum chuckled, "Oh, please don't fight,
My beauty shines through day and night!"

In quirky pots, their tales unwind,
A conga line of leaves they find.
With laughter echoing in the breeze,
These plant pals tease with a leafish tease.

While whispers twirl, and shadows dance,
They celebrate their leafy chance.
With a wink from a nearby twine,
Layers of life, they intertwine.

Sun-Kissed Resilience

In the heat of noon, they gather 'round,
Succulents chirp in a playful sound.
With every ray, they flex and bloom,
Sheltering laughs in their spiky room.

A tender sage with a heart so bold,
Told tales of summer, stories retold.
While prickly pear shared a funny tale,
Of how they survived a giant snail!

In the sun-kissed warmth, they find delight,
Their quirky lives a comical sight.
With laughter sprouting, a joyful cheer,
These resilient greens have nothing to fear.

As twilight descends and shadows stretch,
They join as one, a silly sketch.
In a world of plants, so diverse and bright,
Their sun-kissed bond brings pure delight.

Tales of the Resilient Foliage

In a pot so small and round,
A cactus shakes, no dance profound.
It sways with joy, a spiky cheer,
Sipping sun, it has no fear.

Oregano joined the leafy crew,
Joking about the prickly view.
'At least you're safe!' the basil said,
With dreams of salad in its head.

The aloe laughed, so cool and green,
'Precious me, the soothing queen!'
'You think you got it hard?' it said,
'Try healing cuts and endless dread.'

But every leaf, both waxy and slick,
Knows a dance, a funny trick.
In this garden, laughter's king,
Joyful tales of foliage sing.

The Musical Essence of Cacti

In the desert, notes arise,
A symphony that fills the skies.
With every prick, they play a tune,
Underneath the blazing moon.

The jackrabbits tap their feet,
Humming with the cactus beat.
Each thorn a little drumstick,
Creating rhythms oh so slick.

The creosote bush joins the fun,
While agave shines, the starry one.
Together they form a quirky band,
Making music, oh so grand!

In the back, the lizards croon,
Joining in from afternoon.
'We're not just scaly, we groove too!'
A concert for the desert crew.

Hymn of the Succulent Haven

In sunlit nooks, a choir grows,
With leaves that dance, and laughter flows.
The succulents sway, a raucous tune,
Underneath the watchful moon.

'Let's gather round,' the jade called out,
'A funny tale without a doubt!'
But the prickly pear was sharp and wise,
'Watch your tongue, or meet your demise!'

The stonecrop snickered, 'You're all too tense!'
'It's just a joke, let's not take offense!'
With chuckles here and chuckles there,
They celebrated without a care.

So in this patch, where laughter reigns,
Every leaf knows the joy it gains.
In their own quirky, leafy way,
They sing their hymn of a glorious day.

Storytelling with Sharp Leaves

Once upon a sunny plot,
Lies a cactus with tales, a lot.
'The desert's rough,' it grumbled low,
'But I've got stories for the show!'

The agave stood, all tall and proud,
'Oh please, don't speak too loud!'
'You might scare off the eager sun,
And spoil our chance to have some fun!'

Together they weave a funny tale,
Of winds that twist and rains that fail.
Each leaf a line, each thorn a jest,
In their sharpness, they found their best.

So gather 'round, from big to small,
For the sharp-leaved story, a delight for all.
In this garden, prickly and bright,
Every punchline lands with pure delight.

www.ingramcontent.com/pod-product-compliance
Lightning Source LLC
Chambersburg PA
CBHW070330120526
44590CB00017B/2845